"9Marks, as a ministry, has taken basic biblic[...] [...]o
the hands of pastors. I am unaware of any o[...] [...]y
helps Christians understand God's plan for [...] [...]e
studies in my own congregation."

Jeramie Rinne, Senior Pastor, Sanibel Community Church, Fort Meyers, Florida

"9Marks has done local church pastors an incredible service by writing these study guides. Clear, biblical, and practical, they introduce the biblical basis for a healthy church. But more importantly, they challenge and equip church members to be part of the process of improving their own church's health. The studies work for individual, small group, and larger group settings. I have used them for the last year at my own church and appreciate how easy they are to adapt to my own setting. I don't know of anything else like them. Highly recommended!"

Michael Lawrence, Senior Pastor, Hinson Baptist Church, Portland, Oregon; author, *Biblical Theology in the Life of the Church*

"This is a Bible study that is actually rooted in the Bible and involves actual study. In the 9Marks Healthy Church Study Guides series a new standard has been set for personal theological discovery and corresponding personal application. Rich exposition, compelling questions, and clear syntheses combine to give a guided tour of ecclesiology—the theology of the church. I know of no better curriculum for generating understanding of and involvement in the church than this. It will be a welcome resource in our church for years to come."

Rick Holland, Senior Pastor, Mission Road Bible Church, Prairie Village, Kansas

"In America today we have the largest churches in the history of our nation, but the least amount of impact for Christ's kingdom. Slick marketing and finely polished vision statements are a foundation of sand. The 9Marks Healthy Church Study Guides series is a refreshing departure from church-growth materials toward an in-depth study of God's word that will equip God's people with his vision for his church. These study guides will lead local congregations to abandon secular methodologies for church growth and instead rely on Christ's principles for developing healthy, God-honoring assemblies."

Carl J. Broggi, Senior Pastor, Community Bible Church, Beaufort, South Carolina; President, Search the Scriptures Radio Ministry

"Anyone who loves Jesus will love what Jesus loves. The Bible clearly teaches that Jesus loves the church. He knows about and cares for individual churches and wants them to be spiritually healthy and vibrant. Not only has Jesus laid down his life for the church but he has also given many instructions in his word regarding how churches are to live and function in the world. This series of Bible studies by 9Marks shows how Scripture teaches these things. Any Christian who works through this curriculum, preferably with other believers, will be helped to see in fresh ways the wisdom, love, and power of God in establishing the church on earth. These studies are biblical, practical, and accessible. I highly recommend this curriculum as a useful tool that will help any church embrace its calling to display the glory of God to a watching world."

Thomas Ascol, Executive Director, Founders Ministries; Pastor, Grace Baptist Church, Cape Coral, Florida

9MARKS HEALTHY CHURCH STUDY GUIDES

Built upon the Rock: The Church

Hearing God's Word: Expositional Preaching

The Whole Truth about God: Biblical Theology

God's Good News: The Gospel

Real Change: Conversion

Reaching the Lost: Evangelism

Committing to One Another: Church Membership

Guarding One Another: Church Discipline

Growing One Another: Discipleship in the Church

Leading One Another: Church Leadership

Talking to God: Prayer

Sending and Going Together: Missions

TALKING
TO GOD:
PRAYER

Alex Duke
Mark Dever, General Editor
Jonathan Leeman, Managing Editor

HEALTHY CHURCH STUDY GUIDES

WHEATON, ILLINOIS

Talking to God: Prayer

© 2024 by 9Marks

Published by Crossway
1300 Crescent Street
Wheaton, Illinois 60187

Cover design: Dual Identity

First printing 2024

Trade paperback ISBN: 978-1-4335-8819-8
ePub ISBN: 978-1-4335-8822-8

Crossway is a publishing ministry of Good News Publishers.

CH		32	31	30	29	28	27	26	25	24
14	13	12	11	10	9	8	7	6	5	4	3	2	1

CONTENTS

INTRODUCTION

What does the local church mean to you?

Maybe you love your church. You love the people. You love the preaching and the singing. You can't wait to show up on Sunday, and you cherish fellowship with other church members throughout the week.

Then again, maybe your church is just a place you show up to a couple times a month. You sneak in late, duck out early.

We at 9Marks are convinced that the local church is where God means to display his glory to the nations. And we want to help you catch this vision, together with your whole church.

The *9Marks Healthy Church Study Guides* are a series of six- or seven-week studies on each of the "nine marks of a healthy church" plus one introductory study. These marks are the core convictions of our ministry. To provide a quick introduction and biblical defense of this particular mark, corporate prayer, we've included a condensed chapter from the new edition of Mark Dever's book *Nine Marks of a Healthy Church*. We don't claim that these marks are the only important things about the church. But we do believe that they are biblical and therefore helpful for churches.

So, in these studies, we're going to work through the biblical foundations and practical application of each mark. The twelve studies are:

- *Built upon the Rock: The Church* (the introductory series)
- *Hearing God's Word: Expositional Preaching*
- *The Whole Truth About God: Biblical Theology*
- *God's Good News: The Gospel*
- *Reaching the Lost: Evangelism*
- *Real Change: Conversion*
- *Committing to One Another: Church Membership*

- *Guarding One Another: Church Discipline*
- *Growing One Another: Discipleship in the Church*
- *Leading One Another: Church Leadership*
- *Talking to God: Prayer*
- *Sending and Going Together: Missions*

Each session of these studies takes a close look at one or more passages of Scripture and considers how to apply it to the life of your congregation. We hope they are equally appropriate for Sunday schools, small groups, and other contexts where a group of two to two hundred people can gather to discuss God's word.

These studies are mainly driven by observation, interpretation, and application questions, so get ready to speak up! We also hope that these studies provide opportunities for people to reflect together on their experiences in the church, whatever those experiences may be.

The study you are now holding is called *Talking to God*. It focuses not on personal, private prayer but on the role of corporate, public prayer. Its goal is simple: to encourage churches to devote much time to praying together—in confession and lament, in praise and petition.

Are you ready?

HOW TO PRAY TOGETHER AS A LOCAL CHURCH

By Mark Dever

(Adapted from "Mark Eight" in Nine Marks of a Healthy Church*)*

First-time visitors to our congregation often comment on how much time we spend praying together and sitting silently as others lead in prayer.

In many ways, this practice of prayer should not surprise us. From the first Christians on, praying together is a pattern in the New Testament. The first Christians met to pray (Acts 1:14, 24; 2:42). One of the results of God's pouring out his Spirit on his people at Pentecost was that people met to pray. The circumstances of the prayers in the New Testament vary—offered inside or outside, at various hours of the day and night, sometimes with singing, sometimes with fasting, sometimes kneeling, sometimes with eyes or hands uplifted or laying hands on someone. This great variety seems to illustrate the biblical command to pray without ceasing, through a variety of circumstances (1 Thess. 5:17). I believe this great variety applies to the practice of prayer in the local church. People can be legalistic about particular ways to pray, as if prayer can take only one form. But many of the differences in how churches pray are not problematic, but are simply wonderful reflections of the unique aspects of different congregations' individual characters.

We can, however, make some statements about prayer that apply to *every* church. For the rest of this chapter, I make a number of those statements.

Our public prayer life together as a church should grow out of our individual prayer lives. God's instruction in 1 Thessalonians 5:17 to pray without ceasing should encourage us to set aside some time daily to pray. All the basic aspects of prayer should be in our personal prayer time—praising God for who he is, thanking him for what he has done, confessing who we are and what we've done, and making requests for ourselves and for others. Sometimes people remember this with the acronym ACTS—Adoration, Confession, Thanksgiving, Supplication.

You can integrate *what you pray about* and *who you pray for* when you're in the privacy of your home with the prayer life of the whole congregation. Consider studying in your personal times the passage of Scripture that is going to be preached on the following Lord's Day. Let your requests to God for Elizabeth and Bob and Joe and the other members of your church be shaped by the passage of Scripture. This can also help you pray for others that you don't know well, and it works to prepare your heart for the message to come from that part of God's Word.

Consider praying through your church's membership directory. At Capitol Hill Bapist Church (CHBC), we have a directory that lists all the members. Special sections in the back list former interns and staff so our members know where they are now. There is a section for all the children of members of the church. And one for our supported workers. Because our directory has about sixty pages, it can easily be prayed through monthly by praying through two pages a day. That's what I've done myself and encourage others to do. If we love one another, as we're commanded to do (John 13:35; 1 Thess. 3:12; 2 Thess. 1:3), and have covenanted to do as members, surely that will include praying for each other (James 5:16).

Some of our practices in prayer will vary over time. Just as circumstances varied in the New Testament, they vary in churches today. For example, thirty years ago our church was much smaller and many of our members were older; that had implications for how often we could meet to pray and what time of day we could meet. One newer prayer meeting is hosted by some of the members of the church for the conversion of international students; they meet on Sunday afternoons. Our churchwide prayer meeting used to meet on Wednesday nights, but now we meet on Sunday nights. At times in the life of our church, we've had special meetings for extra prayer, like when we chose our first set of elders. After our nation was attacked in 2001, we hosted a special public meeting. The enduring fact is that we give ourselves in biblical prayers to God for his work here and around the world; there is great liberty in exactly how we do that as a local church.

Some specific words can be especially helpful in leading a church well in prayer. For example, using the plural *we* in the prayers we offer aloud around each other is exampled for us when Jesus taught us to pray "*our* Father." When you or I lead in prayer publicly, we need to remember that we're not just having our own personal devotionals out in public with others listening in; rather, we have the opportunity to lead a whole group of people into the presence of our heavenly Father. In such a position, we would rarely use the word *I*. We would almost always refer to "we" and "our" precisely because we intend to speak to God not simply for matters that concern us as individuals, but for matters that concern the church as a whole. So we pray for *our* joy, not my joy; for *our* work, not my work. We find matters of common concern and interest, and together we go to God in prayer, with one person leading by voicing concerns on behalf of the entire congregation.

Now if *we* is the "hand," as it were, of the one leading in prayer, we the congregation verbally "take the leader's hand" when we say "Amen" at the conclusion of the prayer. *Amen* is Hebrew for "this is true" or "I agree." This is where we get to verbally own, to all those who can hear us, that this prayer is not simply the prayer of the one who verbalized it, but that it is our prayer too. We say "Amen" to it, we agree with what has been prayed, and we publicly accept and affirm this as representing us to God.

In the churches I once visited in China, the declaration of "Amen!" at the conclusion of prayers sounded like claps of thunder. One brother would pray for quite a while, leading you to wonder whether people were really paying attention. But then at the conclusion of the prayer, everyone would clearly and emphatically "own" the prayer as soon as it was concluded with a loud, "Amen." No one could be in any doubt about the unity that such praying represented. That unity is what we're supposed to convey and experience in the local church as we pray together in a way that shows that *we know* that we are praying together. The offer of the plural and the acceptance of the prayer by a clear "Amen" help our church to pray together better.

Different kinds of public prayers help us as a local church. Some churches may have long, spontaneous prayers by a pastor or another member. Others may have various short, planned prayers, as in some church's written liturgies. At CHBC, our longer public prayers tend to be planned and written out, whereas our shorter public prayers tend to be spontaneous. Both kinds of prayers serve our life together well.

Our longer, planned prayers in our Sunday morning services are opportunities to give careful, sustained, reverent, worshipful, hopeful attention to the attributes of God, to his goodness to us, to our sins or our needs, or to gospel work elsewhere. In the prayers in the Old Testament Prophets, the audience of the prayers often switches back and forth from God to the people hearing (or reading) the prayer, and back again. In public prayer, that is understandable. We have to realize that part of what we're doing when we open our mouth in public is teaching others, otherwise leaders wouldn't need a microphone and the congregation wouldn't need to listen.

Some people are surprised at the thought of preparing a prayer ahead of time. They have learned to associate spontaneity with sincerity and preparation with formalism and even hypocrisy. While these are certainly dangers, they aren't inevitable. Preparation does not necessitate insincerity.

Robert Baillie recounts one of the days of prayer that he attended during the Westminster Assembly. "Dr. Twisse having commenced the service with a short prayer, Mr. [Stephen] Marshall prayed large two hours, most divinely confessing the sins of the members of the Assembly, in a wonderful, pathetick [meaning "moving"], and prudent way. After, Mr. Arrowsmith preached an hour, then a psalm;

after which, Mr. Vines prayed nearly two hours, Mr. Palmer preached an hour, and Mr. Seaman prayed nearly two hours, then a psalm. Mr. Henderson then spoke of the evils of the time, and how they were to be remedied, and Dr. Twisse closed the service with a short prayer and blessing."[1] These pastors would prepare for their prayers as much as they would prepare for their sermons.

Pastors or members giving attention and thought to what they will pray about beforehand in no way indicates insincerity in prayer! The care we take in preparing to lead in prayer helps us do this well. It usually takes me about forty-five minutes to prepare the pastoral prayer or one of the other longer prayers in our morning service.

But spontaneous prayers can have much to offer too. They are flexible. We can respond to something we've just learned. We can pray about more different separate events or situations or people. At CHBC our shorter prayers of intercession on Sunday evenings aren't prepared, because the people I ask to lead them aren't given any advance notice. People who might be reluctant to lead in public from the front are much more willing to lead in brief prayers from their seats. Letting someone know that I'm calling on him before I or someone else shares the request allows that person to note down names and particulars, and then, when the time comes, to lead us in brief, direct prayers of petition to God. The variety of people sharing and praying, the variety of matters prayed about, and the brevity of the prayers help us to cover a wide variety in a comparatively short time. So different kinds of prayers—long and short, planned and spontaneous—help us as a local church.

One of our longer prayers on Sunday morning is directed specifically toward praising God. Jesus taught his followers to begin their prayer, "Hallowed be your name." In Psalm 145 David specifically extols and commends God, reflecting on his grace and mercy and goodness. It is good for us to hear prayers of praise, inspired and uninspired. There is so much good to say about God! And it is wonderful to say it back to him. Consider this past week. Did you give much time to thinking about God? Did you recognize and praise him as the one and only

---

[1] *Robert Baillie's Letters*, 2:18–19, cited by James Reid, *Memoirs of the Westminster Divines* (Edinburgh: Banner of Truth, 1982) vol. 2, 77–78.

self-existing God? No one made him. No one could, because he was before everyone else. He alone is everywhere. He has all power and authority. He is the almighty God! He is the Lord Most High! He is the sovereign Lord, the Ancient of Days, avenging and awesome, blessed and compassionate, gracious and eternal, faithful and holy, Creator and forgiver. He is the God of comfort and glory, of heaven and earth, of justice and love, of peace and truth.

Not only do we praise God, the Father of our Lord Jesus Christ, for his character, but we *thank* him both for his character in himself and for what he has done for us: supremely, he has saved us! This is what the choirs in heaven are doing in Revelation, day and night: "Worthy are you, our Lord and God / to receive glory and honor and power, / for you created all things, / and by your will they existed and were created" (Rev. 4:11). The point of so many prayers in the Bible is simply to praise God. Acts 4:24–30 is an example.

> And when they heard it, they lifted their voices together to God and said, "Sovereign Lord, who made the heaven and the earth and the sea and everything in them, who through the mouth of our father David, your servant, said by the Holy Spirit,
>
> > 'Why did the Gentiles rage,
> >   and the peoples plot in vain?
> > The kings of the earth set themselves,
> >   and the rulers were gathered together,
> > against the Lord and against his Anointed'—
>
> for truly in this city there were gathered together against your holy servant Jesus, whom you anointed, both Herod and Pontius Pilate, along with the Gentiles and the peoples of Israel, to do whatever your hand and your plan had predestined to take place. And now, Lord, look upon their threats and grant to your servants to continue to speak your word with all boldness, while you stretch out your hand to heal, and signs and wonders are performed through the name of your holy servant Jesus."

Although the point of the prayer might appear to be the request in verses 29–30, most of the prayer states the truth about this God they are beseeching. Acts 4:24–28 is all praise and thanks, acknowledging God in his good and sovereign actions. We remember that these particular praying believers were scared. Peter had just been arrested. They may have been afraid to meet together. Yet rather than spending most of their time interceding, they spent it praising and thanking God.

CONCLUSION

Old Testament scholar Alec Motyer said that to abandon prayer is to embrace atheism.[2] But, practically speaking, isn't that what too many churches have done today? How much time is spent in prayer in the average evangelical church service today? Do we consider how we are weakening ourselves and our witness when we do that? If we're not gathered around God, why are we gathering at all?

One friend has called prayer "reality attacks." Spending time together in prayer to God reminded the Christians in Acts 4 that the sovereign was not the government who could harass Peter and John, but rather the God who was above *all* governments! The more Christianity is openly despised by the world around us, the more we will need the "reality attacks" of prayer to remind us of what will be the reality on the last day.

Moses Hall's courage was fueled by prayer. Hall was an African-Jamaican pastor in Jamaica in the early 1800s. Some African Christians who were enslaved in Jamaica were gathering regularly to pray, even though such prayer meetings were outlawed by their masters. This is an account of one occasion.

> Determined to put an end to slave meetings [in Jamaica], some slave owners broke up a prayer meeting being led by a slave named David, one of [Moses] Hall's assistants. They seized David, murdered him, cut off his head, and placed it on a pole in the center of the village as a warning to the other slaves.
>
> Eerily like crucifying Jesus as a public warning.
>
> They dragged Moses Hall up to the grisly object.
>
> "Now, Moses Hall, whose head is that?" the leader of the murderers asked.
>
> "David's," Moses replied.

---

[2] Alec Motyer, *Psalms of the Day: A New Devotional Translation* (Fern, Ross-shire, UK: Christian Focus, 2016), 246.

"Do you know why he is up here?"

"For praying, Sir," said Moses.

"No more of your prayer meetings," he said. "If we catch you at it, we shall serve you as we have served David."

As the crowd watched, Moses knelt beside the pole and said, "Let us pray." The other black [Christians] gathered around and knelt with him as he prayed for the salvation of [David's] murderers.[3]

When we pray, we call on the God of the universe to help us glorify him. And we remind ourselves of who it is that we should really fear and regard and reverence and love.

Do you understand a little more of how God may use the time we spend praying together as a church? Of course, much of the way God uses prayer will be in undramatic ways. Over the years, more than one member has communicated thanks for how our church has taught them to pray. Perhaps they're trying to teach their children, and they remember back to what they have heard on a Sunday night. Or maybe they're asked to pray at a public event, and they remember back to how they've heard us lead in prayer on Sunday morning. Perhaps they've been in a dry period spiritually, and they simply have been longing for the kind of guided spiritual quiet time that our Sunday morning services are for them, like physical therapy for your soul, when you've been wounded or hurt or exhausted spiritually.

I relish such testimonies. A church that is known for its prayer life is not indulging in self-promotion but in God-promotion. We realize that every time we pray, we are advertising our own inadequacy. We need somebody else. Moses Hall wasn't trumpeting his own courage— he was openly displaying his utter reliance on God, who was entirely up to the task! When we spend time together in prayer, we put to death wrong legalistic or moralistic ideas of Christianity. In advertising our neediness, we separate the gospel from the kind of "positive confession" false teaching that is all too prevalent today. We lift up the God who has faithfully pursued us in amazing love in Christ. We show that God is our hope. As our prayer advertises our dependence upon God and the fact that God is dependable, our prayers become praise. And such prayer should and will mark a healthy church.

---

[3] Mark Sidwell, *Free Indeed: Heroes of Black Christian History* (Greenville, SC: BJU Press, 2001), 29.

WEEK 1
CHURCHES SHOULD PRAY

GETTING STARTED

1. How much prayer did you hear in your church this past Sunday? Based on your answer, would you say your church prays too little, too much, or just enough? Defend your answer.

2. In what sense is corporate prayer distinct from individual prayer?

What should churches do when they gather? Several things immediately come to mind: they should sing, they should take the Lord's Supper and baptize, they should hear a sermon from God's word, and, of course, they should pray.

Our sermons, songs, and sacraments receive a lot of attention. But what about our prayers? Do our churches give significant attention to their prayers? Are they planned and prepared just like other elements of our gatherings? Or are they rushed and short, perfunctory and transitional?

MAIN IDEA
Churches should spend significant time praying together.

DIGGING IN
Though Jesus promises to build his church as early as Matthew 16, a local church doesn't appear until Peter's preaching in Acts 2. He preaches the word and shares the gospel of Jesus Christ, and the Holy Spirit moves in the hearts of many. In a single day, it seems, more than three thousand people repented, believed, and were baptized (Acts 2:41).

What happened next? Those who stayed in Jerusalem became the first local church. Here's how Luke summarizes their life together:

> And they devoted themselves to the apostles' teaching and the fellowship, to the breaking of bread and the prayers. And awe came upon every soul, and many wonders and signs were being done through the apostles. And all who believed were together and had all things in common. And they were selling their possessions and belongings and distributing the proceeds to all, as any had need. And day by day, attending the temple together and breaking bread in their homes, they received their food with glad and generous hearts, praising God and having favor with all the people. And the Lord added to their number day by day those who were being saved. (Acts 2:42–47)

There's much that could be said about this summary of the corporate Christian life. But for now (and throughout the rest of this study guide) we'll focus on a single phrase: "They devoted themselves to . . . the prayers" (2:42). Something similar happens later in Acts 4 after Peter and John get released from prison. How does the church respond? They pray (4:23–30).

Churches today should follow this pattern of prayer. They should be "devoted" to prayer. They should gather together and pray as both a regular rhythm of life (Acts 2:42–47) and a response to unique circumstances that are troubling, praiseworthy, and everything in between (Acts 4:23–31).

In doing so, they will follow in the footsteps of the people of God throughout the ages. How do we know this is true? Consider the Psalms. The book of Psalms is a collection of corporate confessions that cover the emotional range of our lives with God. Though some were written by individuals at specific moments in their lives, over time they were all adapted by the nation of Israel to be used in corporate worship at the temple. Before anything else, the book of Psalms is a hymnbook. And as a hymnbook, it shapes how God's people address him with their confessions, requests, and praises.

The goal of this study guide is to investigate various biblical examples—from both the Old and New Testaments—that should shape how our churches pray.

In sum, our corporate prayers shouldn't always be short and sweet; sometimes, they should be long and deep. They should praise God's character, confess our sins, lament the world's fallenness, and communicate our dependence on God to meet all our needs—from our daily bread to evangelistic fruit, godly leadership, and the establishment of qualified church leaders. Churches should pray.

1. Why should churches be devoted to praying together?

2. Every church prays. But what does it look like for a church to not be devoted to praying together?

3. Have you seen churches that model this devotion well? What did prayer look like in those gatherings?

4. What are the long-term effects of neglecting prayer within the church?

5. What are the long-term effects of regularly praying as a church?

6. Have you ever thought of the Psalms as a corporate worship guide for the people of God? How does that change how you approach the book?

WEEK 2
CHURCHES SHOULD
CONFESS

GETTING STARTED

Many Christians in recent years have discussed the legitimacy of corporate confessions for the sin of previous generations. How can a group of people confess sins that they didn't actually commit? Is this even possible?

Those are worthwhile questions. But answering them is not the goal of this week. The goal of this week is to hold up a different kind of corporate confession, that is, the habit of praying with your church about your own sins and celebrating—together—God's certain and ever-present mercy in Christ.

MAIN IDEA

Churches should confess their sins together.

DIGGING IN

The book of Ezra tells the story of Israelite exiles who rebuilt God's temple. At least that's what's happening on the surface. More significantly, the book of Ezra tells the story of God fulfilling his promises to his exiled people by bringing them back and establishing them once again in their land. Lest we forget, the Israelites deserved precisely none of this. It was all grace.

Ezra 2 details the list of exiles who God will use to restore his temple. Unfortunately, the people ignore God by marrying idolaters. As their commissioned leader, Ezra is forced to address their sin. So what does he do? In Ezra 9–10, he doesn't scold them, nor does he preach a sermon to them. Instead, he cries out to God on their behalf. He *prays*.

This week, we'll focus on Ezra's prayer as an example for what corporate confession should look like. Below is Ezra's prayer of confession in full. Read it slowly, perhaps even as a prayer for yourself:

> O my God, I am ashamed and blush to lift my face to you, my God, for our iniquities have risen higher than our heads, and our guilt has mounted up to the heavens. From the days of our fathers to this day we have been in great guilt. And for our iniquities we, our kings, and our priests have been given into the hand of the kings of the lands, to the sword, to captivity, to plundering, and to utter shame, as it is today. But now for a brief moment favor has been shown by the Lord our God, to leave us a remnant and to give us a secure hold within his holy place, that our God may brighten our eyes and grant us a little reviving in our slavery. For we are slaves. Yet our God has not forsaken us in our slavery, but has extended to us his steadfast love before the kings of Persia, to grant us some reviving to set up the house of our God, to repair its ruins, and to give us protection in Judea and Jerusalem. And now, O our God, what shall we say after this? For we have forsaken your commandments, which you commanded by your servants the prophets, saying, "The land that you are entering, to take possession of it, is a land impure with the impurity of the peoples of the lands, with their abominations that have filled it from end to end with their uncleanness. Therefore do not give your daughters to their sons, neither take their daughters for your sons, and never seek their peace or prosperity, that you may be strong and eat the good of the land and leave it for an inheritance to your children forever." And after all that has come upon us for our evil deeds and for our great guilt, seeing that you, our God, have punished us less than our iniquities deserved and have given us such a remnant as this, shall we break your commandments again and intermarry with the peoples who practice these abominations? Would you not be angry with us until you consumed us, so that there should be no remnant, nor any to escape? O Lord, the God of Israel, you are just, for we are left a remnant that has escaped, as it is today. Behold, we are before you in our guilt, for none can stand before you because of this. (Ezra 9:6–15)

1. Ezra's prayer is context specific. It's the specific response of a specific group of people for their specific sins. In your own words, write out the context.

2. How did reading this passage make you feel? In what ways did it convict you? In what ways did it encourage you?

3. In light of this passage, what do you think the elements of a corporate prayer of confession are?

4. Now read Ezra 10. What does this tell you about the proper congregational response to a corporate confession of sin? Which aspects of their response are cultural and which transcend culture?

5. In light of this session, write out your own prayer of confession. Yes, an individual prayer of confession is different than a corporate one, but the practice is still fruitful. If you need some prodding, consider using the Ten Commandments or the Beatitudes as a rubric or look to Daniel 9:1–19. It's generally helpful to let Scripture guide your prayers.

6. Prayers of confession are often followed by an assurance of pardon because the goal of confession is restoration (1 John 1:9). Do you see one in Ezra 9? Write one for the prayer you wrote out.

WEEK 3
CHURCHES SHOULD
LAMENT

GETTING STARTED

1. What is a lament? How is it different than a confession?

2. What passages come to mind that address this topic of lament?

Neal Woollard helpfully explains,

> The world is not as it should be—and we feel it. From natural disasters to school shootings to personal tragedies, we've all been affected by the brokenness of a fallen world. We yearn for Jesus' return to right all wrongs and renew our world, freeing us from the chaos and grief that accompanies deep suffering.[4]

Sometimes, our yearning is because of our sins or others' sins. But often, we experience suffering and sorrow simply because we're human beings in a fallen world. What do we do in these moments? Confession isn't quite the right response. So what else is there?

There's lament. Contrary to popular belief, "lament" is not simply a synonym for "complain" or "talk about sad stuff." It is more specific than that. Borrowing from one author, we could say that a lament is a "prayer in pain that leads to trust."[5] Each element of that definition is important: it's a prayer, which means it's addressed to God. But it's a prayer that is born out of suffering and pain. And finally, it's a prayer given in suffering that aims not at the expulsion of anger but

---

[4] Neal Woollard, "Why We Added a Prayer of Lament to Our Sunday Gathering," 9Marks, June 20, 2018, https://www.9marks.org/.
[5] Mark Vroegop, *Dark Clouds, Deep Mercy: Discovering the Grace of Lament* (Wheaton, IL: Crossway, 2019), 28.

the expansion of trust. That's absolutely vital to remember. In the Bible, laments speak our sorrow out loud, but they do so in order to end up at worship.

MAIN IDEA
Churches should lament together.

DIGGING IN
According to Woollard,

> The Bible is full of laments. In the Old Testament, almost a third of Israel's songbook is devoted to psalms of lament, both corporate and individual. Israel's wisdom literature offers the story of Job's honest protests to the Lord amid his tragedy. Lamentations is a tear-drenched book entirely dedicated to the cries of God's people as they process the greatest catastrophe in their history and ask for deliverance despite their sin. In the New Testament, we witness Jesus lamenting Jerusalem's future doom and then his own path of doom in the garden. We see missionaries like Paul crying over his lost brothers of Israel. Even in Revelation, the martyred saints cry out "How long, oh Lord?" as they await their vindication. Lament is ingrained into the culture of Jesus' people and will be until he returns.[6]

So, too, should lament have a place in our local churches. There are many biblical examples we could appeal to.[7] For now, we'll focus on just one, Psalm 44:

> O God, we have heard with our ears,
>   our fathers have told us,
> what deeds you performed in their days,
>   in the days of old:
>
> you with your own hand drove out the nations,
>   but them you planted;
> you afflicted the peoples,
>   but them you set free;

---

[6] Woollard, "Why We Added a Prayer of Lament."
[7] See, for example, Psalm 12, 13, 44, 58, 60, 74, 77, 79, 80, 83, 85, 89, 90, 94, 123, 126, 129, and 130, and the book of Lamentations.

for not by their own sword did they win the land,
    nor did their own arm save them,
but your right hand and your arm,
    and the light of your face,
for you delighted in them.

You are my King, O God;
    ordain salvation for Jacob!

Through you we push down our foes;
    through your name we tread down those who rise up against us.

For not in my bow do I trust,
    nor can my sword save me.

But you have saved us from our foes
    and have put to shame those who hate us.

In God we have boasted continually,
    and we will give thanks to your name forever. *Selah*

But you have rejected us and disgraced us
    and have not gone out with our armies.

You have made us turn back from the foe,
    and those who hate us have gotten spoil.

You have made us like sheep for slaughter
    and have scattered us among the nations.

You have sold your people for a trifle,
    demanding no high price for them.

You have made us the taunt of our neighbors,
    the derision and scorn of those around us.

You have made us a byword among the nations,
    a laughingstock among the peoples.

All day long my disgrace is before me,
    and shame has covered my face

TALKING TO GOD

at the sound of the taunter and reviler,
   at the sight of the enemy and the avenger.

All this has come upon us,
   though we have not forgotten you,
   and we have not been false to your covenant.

Our heart has not turned back,
   nor have our steps departed from your way;

yet you have broken us in the place of jackals
   and covered us with the shadow of death.

If we had forgotten the name of our God
   or spread out our hands to a foreign god,

would not God discover this?
   For he knows the secrets of the heart.

Yet for your sake we are killed all the day long;
   we are regarded as sheep to be slaughtered.

Awake! Why are you sleeping, O Lord?
   Rouse yourself! Do not reject us forever!

Why do you hide your face?
   Why do you forget our affliction and oppression?

For our soul is bowed down to the dust;
   our belly clings to the ground.

Rise up; come to our help!
   Redeem us for the sake of your steadfast love!

1. As best you can tell, what are the circumstances behind this corporate lament?

2. What is the function of the first eight verses?

3. What specific accusations does the lament make against the Lord?

4. What specific actions does the lament call the Lord to?

5. Even amid the complaints, where do sparks of trust in God show up?

6. What aspects of God's character does the psalm focus on?

7. Have you ever prayed to God like this? If you have, what kind of fruit have you seen from these prayers? If you haven't, what has prevented you?

8. Try to write out a prayer of lament.

9. What kinds of situations should prod our churches to pray corporate laments?

WEEK 4
CHURCHES SHOULD
PETITION

GETTING STARTED

1. What kinds of needs should churches pray about during their corporate gatherings? Should we prioritize some needs over others? Why or why not?

2. Does your church have a prayer meeting? If so, what is it like? If not, do you wish you had one?

In one sense, every prayer is a petition. It acknowledges that we are in need and the Lord is able to meet those needs. Whether he decides to is up to him. But every request acknowledges our limitations and his limitless ability.

So what needs should we pray for? The Bible doesn't specifically answer this question. After all, Paul tells us, we ought to "pray without ceasing" (1 Thess. 5:17). So it seems nothing is out of bounds. But sometimes, a church's prayer list can become little more than a list of sick relatives and which former members—long forgotten by most of the congregation—are on the mission field.

Should that suffice?

MAIN IDEA

Churches should petition the Lord to meet their needs, especially (but not only) spiritual needs.

DIGGING IN

Here's an incomplete list of things churches either pray about or are told to pray about in the New Testament:

- For boldness after Peter and John were released from prison (Acts 4:23–31)
- For the men who were chosen as deacons (Acts 6:6)
- For Peter, who was suffering in prison (Acts 12:5, 12)
- For Paul and Barnabas, when the church at Antioch sent them out (Acts 13:3)
- For fruit from Paul's ministry (Rom. 15:30–33; Phil. 1:19; Col. 4:2–4; 1 Thess. 5:25; 2 Thess. 3:1; Philem. 22)
- For God rescuing Paul from a difficult situation (2 Cor. 1:8–11).
- For any needs or anxieties (Phil. 4:6)
- For "all people," but especially "kings and all who are in high positions" so that it may be easier to live as a Christian and spread the gospel (1 Tim. 2:1–3)
- For suffering and sickness (James 5:13–14)

Read through each of those passages to get a sense of the many ways in which prayer shows up in the life of New Testament churches.

1. In light of the list above, should a church privilege certain prayer requests over others?

2. In what context does your church spend considerable amounts of time and focus praying about these things? In those contexts, what do you primarily pray about?

3. One common theme in the New Testament, particularly in the Pauline epistles, is the encouragement to pray for fruitful ministries outside a particular local church. Does your church consistently pray for the growth of the gospel outside its own walls, either locally or globally? If so, how? If not, why not?

4. List as many evangelical churches in your area as you can think of. Start praying for fruit from their ministry. You may even want to encourage your pastors to publicly pray for local ministries as well.

5. List the missionaries your church supports. Do you know enough about them to pray in specific ways for them? If not, get to know them and what they're doing, and let that information shape your prayers.

6. *What positive effects happen in a church that regularly prays for other people's ministries, including other nearby local churches?*

7. *What positive effects happen in a church that regularly prays for specific needs that come up within the body? Read 2 Corinthians 1:8–11 to see a biblical example of this.*

WEEK 5
CHURCHES SHOULD PRAISE

GETTING STARTED

1. What is a prayer of praise? How is it different from the other kinds of prayers we've studied?

2. To what degree should our prayers focus on God?

It's good to confess our sins, to lament over tragedy, and to petition the Lord to meet our needs. But if that's *all* we ever do in our prayers, then we've missed something absolutely crucial. You might even say that we've missed the whole point of prayer: growing in our knowledge and trust of the triune God.

MAIN IDEA

Churches should praise God for who he is, focusing their prayers on all the diverse, beautiful, and praiseworthy aspects of his character.

DIGGING IN

John Onwuchekwa helpfully explains,

> In our prayers of praise, we want to remember what God is like, not just what he's done for us. We're praising him for his attributes and characteristics—his holiness, gentleness, goodness, even his wrath. The wonder of these prayers doesn't come simply from listing off God's attributes, but from unpacking them. . . . We should desire to praise God not generally, but specifically. This helps to minimize the empty phrases people tend to use. It also fills in the gaps where people tend to import their own definitions of God. For example, we praise God for his eternality. Because he exists from everlasting to everlasting, he is God (see Ps. 90:2). He's been on the throne

forever. He has witnessed the birth of every evil ruler. He remembers them as babies. He knows the day they'll be buried. He's never intimidated. They'll come and go, but he will remain on the throne. His position is secure. He never makes a decision out of fear that someone will take his place. His back is never against a wall, which means we can trust he has no ulterior motives for giving us the commands he does.[8]

This is what it sounds like to praise God for his eternality. Onwuchekwa concludes,

Delving into God's attributes means we must pay attention to the attributes of God we sometimes feel tempted to apologize for. Think of God's anger and wrath. When we praise him for those things during corporate worship, we're reminded that God is committed to justice. Wrath isn't a liability. It's proof of his protection. God's anger, directed at sin, reminds us that he is a protector of the weak. His inability to ignore sin and the relentless way he punishes evil is scary because we fear we could easily find ourselves as the objects of his wrath. But for those who take shelter under the protection he has offered through his Son, we realize God's holiness is for our protection, not our punishment.[9]

1. In your own words, what makes a prayer of praise (sometimes called a prayer of adoration) unique?

2. What does it mean to praise God for who he is and not just what he's done?

3. Practically speaking, what is the difference between praising God generally and praising God specifically?

4. List some specific attributes of God—not actions—that deserve our considered reflection through prayer.

5. Pick one attribute and write out a 250-word prayer of praise.

---

[8] John Onwuchekwa, *Prayer: How Praying Together Helps the Church* (Wheaton, IL: Crossway, 2018), 80–81.
[9] Onwuchekwa, *Prayer*, 81.

6. What are the benefits of using this kind of prayer in a local church?

7. What are the negative effects of neglecting this kind of prayer in the church?

WEEK 6
CHURCHES SHOULD BE
UNITED

GETTING STARTED

1. What kind of unity do churches enjoy? What passages come to mind that talk about this?

2. How does corporate prayer lead to unity in times of trial and difficulty?

In times of trouble and suffering, churches lament and stake their hope on the Lord. When sin seems to lurk around every corner, churches confess and enjoy assurance of pardon through Christ. When the needs of members seem unending, churches petition the Lord for help. In every season, churches praise the Lord for who he is, "merciful and gracious, slow to anger, and abounding in steadfast love and faithfulness" (Ex. 34:6). What's the result of all this prayer? Unity.

MAIN IDEA

When churches commit themselves to prayer, they both cultivate and demonstrate the unity that was planned by the Father, purchased by the Son, and sustained by the Spirit.

DIGGING IN

When we try to describe our local churches, "unified" isn't always the first word that comes to mind. But it's the truth: churches are unified. So where did this unity come from? It's not manufactured through sheer effort, and it's certainly not manipulated through superficial similarities between congregants. No; a church's unity is achieved by the triune God.

That's what Jesus prays for in John 17:20–21: "I do not ask for these only, but also for those who will believe in me through their word, that they may all be one, just as you, Father, are in me, and I in you, that they also may be in us, so that the world may believe that you have sent me." In this passage, Jesus is praying not just for his disciples at the time but for all Christians everywhere throughout all time. In fact, the latter is the most immediate application here. So what does this have to do with a local church like yours? The apostle Paul unpacks similar ideas in his letter to the Ephesian church, and his explanation can help us answer this question.

He begins by reminding these Christians of all the various blessings that result from their union with Christ. These saints in Ephesus have been redeemed through Christ's blood and therefore have obtained an inheritance. They've been redeemed by Jesus, love Jesus, and ought to live as the body of Jesus; he is their head, and it's their job to reflect him to the watching world. That's Ephesians 1.

Paul then reminds this church that the Lord saved them individually so that he could build something beautiful corporately. Ephesians 2 displays the beautiful building the Lord is constructing: the first half describes how the bricks got there in the first place, and the second half explains the structure's architectural plans. Look at this passage in detail:

> Therefore remember that at one time you Gentiles in the flesh, called "the uncircumcision" by what is called the circumcision, which is made in the flesh by hands—remember that you were at that time separated from Christ, alienated from the commonwealth of Israel and strangers to the covenants of promise, having no hope and without God in the world. But now in Christ Jesus you who once were far off have been brought near by the blood of Christ. For he himself is our peace, who has made us both one and has broken down in his flesh the dividing wall of hostility by abolishing the law of commandments expressed in ordinances, that he might create in himself one new man in place of the two, so making peace, and might reconcile us both to God in one body through the cross, thereby killing the hostility. And he came and preached peace to you who were far off and peace to those who were near. For through him we both have access in one Spirit to the Father. So then you are no longer strangers

and aliens, but you are fellow citizens with the saints and members of the household of God, built on the foundation of the apostles and prophets, Christ Jesus himself being the cornerstone, in whom the whole structure, being joined together, grows into a holy temple in the Lord. In him you also are being built together into a dwelling place for God by the Spirit. (vv. 11–22)

What an explosive passage. Every local church is a beautiful household full of redeemed and reconciled people. Former strangers, brought home. Former enemies, made friends. That was true of Jews and Gentiles two thousand years ago. And it's true of local churches today.

Paul keeps going. In Ephesians 3:7–12, he describes his testimony and his calling: to preach the gospel to the Gentiles. If you've read Acts, you know that. But he continues on. He has also been given the job of revealing one of God's eternal mysteries. Here's how he explains it:

Of this gospel I was made a minister according to the gift of God's grace, which was given me by the working of his power. To me, though I am the very least of all the saints, this grace was given, to preach to the Gentiles the unsearchable riches of Christ, and to bring to light for everyone what is the plan of the mystery hidden for ages in God, who created all things, so that through the church the manifold wisdom of God might now be made known to the rulers and authorities in the heavenly places. This was according to the eternal purpose that he has realized in Christ Jesus our Lord, in whom we have boldness and access with confidence through our faith in him.

What is the eternal purpose that God jumpstarted in Christ Jesus our Lord? Churches that reflect God's manifold, varied, diverse, unmatched wisdom. The angels and other heavenly authorities can see it now. Can we? We sometimes need help to see this, which is partly why Paul prays for (Eph. 3:14–21) and urges them to maintain the unity of the Spirit that they have as a church, a unity that enables them to accomplish the mission they're all on together (4:1–16).

Thankfully, Christ has given gifts to his church to equip us for this work so that the whole body becomes mature and stable, marked by unity and confident trust in the Son of God. When all this is "working properly" (Eph. 4:16), a local church will grow and build itself up in love.

So what does all this have to do with prayer? In Jamie Dunlop's words, "Unity among God's people glorifies God. That's why Paul calls on the *entire church* in Ephesians 4 to keep the unity of the Spirit through the bond of peace. Praying together is one way that we satisfy this command—it visibly unites us together as God's people."[10]

1. Read through the book of Ephesians. What stands out to you about the unity of the church?

2. How can it be that unity is something we must both "maintain" (Eph. 4:3) and "attain" (4:13)?

3. Imagine a situation that brings disunity to the church—perhaps a nationwide election or a troublesome local event. How might a long history of praying together help a church to stay unified?

4. Can you think of a time where you felt some tension with either your church as a whole or a brother or sister in it? Did you try praying together? If so, what resulted?

5. What things should a church unite around? What things should a church not officially seek to unite around? How do the latter points of disunity demonstrate the power and beauty of things we are united around?

6. As we reach the end of this study on corporate prayer, let's reflect on the questions from the beginning.

- How much prayer did you hear in your church this past Sunday? Would you say your church prays too little, too much, or just enough? Defend your answer.

- In what sense is corporate prayer distinct from individual prayer?

---

[10] Jamie Dunlop, "Class IV: Corporate Prayer," 9Marks, March 1, 2010, https://www.9marks.org/.

TEACHER'S NOTES FOR WEEK 1

DIGGING IN

1. At minimum, it reflects the New Testament model. But try to encourage readers to reflect on the topic more deeply. Corporate prayer also reflects a church's unity, underscores its dependence on God, and teaches new believers how to pray.

2. If a church's gatherings feature less than a few minutes of prayer, it would be hard to argue that it is devoted to prayer. Of course, devotion to prayer relates to more than the duration of prayer, but it's certainly not less.

3. Answers will vary.

4. A few possible answers are that prayerless churches start to believe they are self-sufficient, become spiritually anemic, and focus only on themselves rather than their community or the global church.

5. A few possible answers are that prayerful churches recognize their dependence on God, become spiritually vibrant, and are appropriately concerned with issues outside their immediate perspective and sphere of influence.

6. Help readers see that every psalm is a corporate cry, not just individual supplication.

TEACHER'S NOTES FOR WEEK 2

DIGGING IN

1. The *ESV Study Bible* explains, "Ezra discovers that the Jewish community has mixed with idolatrous non-Jewish groups in religion and in marriage, and he leads the community in an act of repentance and in a systematic separation from the foreign women and their children."[11]

2. Answers will vary.

3. Corporate prayers of confession should include statements about God's holiness, our specific sins, our personal repentance, and God's mercy and steadfast love.

4. A proper congregational response requires agreeing with God about our sins. We cannot minimize or sweep these under the rug. However, most of the aspects of Ezra's prayer are cultural and thus non-binding. For example, genuine repentance does not require a priestly oath (v. 5), a fast (vv.6–7), or gathering at a specific place.

5. Answers will vary.

6. The assurance of pardon is found in Ezra 9:9–15.

---

[11] J. Gordon McConville, study notes for Ezra in *ESV Study Bible* (Wheaton, IL: Crossway, 2008), 1316.

TEACHER'S NOTES FOR WEEK 3

DIGGING IN

1. The *ESV Study Bible* explains,

> This is a hymn for when the people of God as a whole have suffered great calamity at the hands of their enemies and are seeking God's help. The calamity is particularly painful because God has chosen his people, given them a special place, and favored them over their enemies in the past. The hymn's corporate focus is not impersonal, however; each member of the congregation identifies with the whole people by using the singular "I" (vv. 4, 6, 15). When the worshiping congregation sings this, they do more than simply present a request to God. They also remind themselves of their privileged standing with God, of the obligation to faith and holiness that is laid upon them, and of God's unfailing loyalty to his purpose for his people.[12]

2. The song opens by recalling the ways God has favored his people over the Gentiles in the past. It recounts his special provision.

3. You have rejected us (v. 9), disgraced us (v. 9), and left us for dead (v. 9). That's just the beginning. The list is long and covers every phrase from 44:9–14. Then the lament seems to accuse the Lord of hypocrisy in 44:17–22 and ignorance in 44:23–24.

4. This lament calls the Lord to wake up and to no longer hide his face and forget the affliction of his people (vv. 23–24). Then the song culminates in a request for help and redemption (v. 26).

5. The clearest one is the final phrase: God's covenant love is the foundation of the request. Before that, sparks of trust show up in the preamble that recounts God's past faithfulness, especially verse 4 in which the author celebrates God as the King who leads his people.

6. Answers may include his faithfulness (vv. 1–8), justice (v. 20), mercy (v. 26), and omniscience (v. 21).

7–9. Answers will vary.

---

[12] C. John Collins, study notes for the Psalms in *ESV Study Bible* (Wheaton, IL: Crossway, 2008), 991.

TEACHER'S NOTES FOR WEEK 4

DIGGING IN

1. Generally speaking, churches should prioritize prayers about spiritual matters—for example, evangelism, sanctification, church planting, missionaries, and boldness amid persecution—over more mundane issues. This does not mean we should exclude the latter entirely but rather that our prayers should reflect the same emphases as prayers in the New Testament.

2–5. Answers will vary.

6. There are several possible answers. Here are two examples: A church that regularly prays for other ministries will grow in humility because they will realize that the gospel's advance doesn't depend on them. They will also grow in generosity because a humble heart is a generous heart.

7. First and foremost, when churches regularly pray for specific needs within the body, they communicate that the church is not an event but a people. Secondarily, this also teaches Christians to be open and vulnerable about what's going on in their lives. In other words, praying churches incentivize transparency because they allow congregants to participate in the joys of seeing how God answers specific prayer requests in his church.

TEACHER'S NOTES FOR WEEK 5

DIGGING IN

1. A prayer of praise doesn't immediately slip into a prayer of confession that focuses on ourselves or a prayer of thanksgiving that focuses on what God has done. Rather, a prayer of praise looks to who God is in himself. It focuses on his attributes and character. It requires concentration and attention.

2. This means focusing on God's attributes, not actions. God does what he does because of who he is; that's worth asserting and restating. But praising God for his specific actions is not, strictly speaking, the intention of a prayer of praise.

3. Simply listing off a handful of God's attributes is an example of praising him in a general way. Focusing more intently on one or two attributes is an example of praising him in a specific way. Ask readers to share a few examples of these.

4–5. Answers will vary.

6. A church that devotes itself to praising God in prayer will grow in both knowledge and adoration. Their speech about God will become more specific and concrete (as opposed to vague and abstract). As a result, they will be prepared for suffering and trials. They'll also be more likely to respond wisely in conversations with skeptics and seekers.

7. A church that fails to devote itself to praising God in prayer will be at risk of shallow understanding and weak adoration. When sorrow and suffering come, church members may not know what to say beyond abstract platitudes. Furthermore, when they find themselves in evangelistic conversations, they may not be able to address some questions thoughtfully because they haven't dwelt on God's person and work.

TEACHER'S NOTES FOR WEEK 6

DIGGING IN

1. Several passages in Ephesians address unity but chapter 2 is a wonderful place to start. The first half of the chapter is well-known—Paul explains how God saves us as individuals by grace through faith so that no one may boast. But pay close attention to the latter half of the chapter (vv. 11–22). There, Paul describes what kind of corporate body he's building through saved-by-grace individuals.

2. A church's unity has been purchased by Jesus's work (Eph. 2:11–22). It's the fruit of his labor, and it's ours as the church to enjoy. That's why we must "maintain" it. And yet, it's also something we grow into through the church and with the Spirit's help (Eph. 4:1–24). That's why it's something we "attain" to.

Think of it like a marriage. There's no degree of being married; you're either one flesh or you're not. Couples maintain this state simply by remaining married. And yet, their enjoyment of that one-flesh union grows over time as they grow in their relationship. They attain it by loving, forgiving, and showing grace to each other. Scripture speaks like this about a lot of topics. Another example is sanctification. We are "new creations" and "dead to sin" once we come to Christ (2 Cor. 5:17; Rom. 6:2). And yet, we must also "put to death" the deeds of the flesh (Rom. 8:13). If we think of the church as an evangelistic event, a program for Christians, or a religious institution, then this kind of language doesn't make any sense. But when we realize that a church is a people whom God has redeemed and placed beside one another to help each other get to heaven, then these truths become easier to comprehend.

3–4. Answers will vary.

5. The shortest answer is the simplest: we should unite around our statement of faith and church covenant. We should not unite around anything else— a political persuasion, an educational model, an idiosyncratic theological position, a shared assessment of the culture, a common adversary (unless that adversary is the devil!), a particular evangelistic strategy, or a Bible study method. The list could go on and on. Forced agreement on extra-biblical issues is a threat to the purchased unity we already enjoy through Christ.

6. Answers will vary.

9Marks
Building Healthy Churches

9Marks exists to equip church leaders with a biblical vision and practical resources for displaying God's glory to the nations through healthy churches.

To that end, we want to see churches characterized by these nine marks of health:

1. Expositional Preaching
2. Gospel Doctrine
3. A Biblical Understanding of Conversion and Evangelism
4. Biblical Church Membership
5. Biblical Church Discipline
6. A Biblical Concern for Discipleship and Growth
7. Biblical Church Leadership
8. A Biblical Understanding of the Practice of Prayer
9. A Biblical Understanding and Practice of Missions

Find all our Crossway titles and other resources at 9Marks.org.

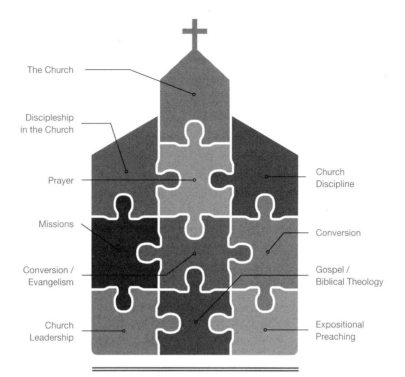

The Church

Discipleship in the Church

Prayer

Missions

Conversion / Evangelism

Church Leadership

Church Discipline

Conversion

Gospel / Biblical Theology

Expositional Preaching

Be sure to check out the rest of the
**9MARKS HEALTHY CHURCH
STUDY GUIDE SERIES**

9Marks Healthy Church Study Guides
is a series of twelve 6–7 week studies
covering the nine distinctives of a
healthy church as laid out in *Nine Marks
of a Healthy Church* by Mark Dever. This
series explores the biblical foundations
of key aspects of the church, helping
Christians live out those realities as
members of a local body.